The Minichefs Cookbook

Claire McAvoy

Grub Street | London

This edition produced for The Book People by
Grub Street, 4 Rainham Close, London SW11 6SS
Email: food@grubstreet.co.uk
Web: www.grubstreet.co.uk

A CIP record for this title is available from the British Library
ISBN 978-1-904943-77-8

Printed and bound in India

How to be part of Minichefs

You can log onto the Minichefs website on
www.minichefs.com and become a part of the
Minichefs community. This site is designed so that you
can send in your recipes from anywhere in the world
and share them with other Minichefs. If you want you
can send a photo of the finished dish or maybe one of
you in action cooking. Also you can email saying which
dishes from the book you have tried out. Tell us if you
liked them or changed them? We will post your reports
on our community page.

Contents

Food for thought A note to parents

Congratulations, by acquiring this book you have taken the first steps to introducing your children to the wonderful world of food.

The idea behind this book is simple. To get as many kids cooking and enjoying real food at the earliest age possible. To encourage parents to spend some quality time with their children being creative and producing a dish that can be enjoyed and shared.

Jamie Oliver has improved the standard of meals in schools, so let's get right back to grass roots and improve those in the home too. Give parents and their children the knowledge and understanding of good food with a bright, fun and informative book.

I firmly believe that developing children's cooking skills at an early age will change their whole attitude to food for life. They gain the confidence to explore different ingredients through taste, touch and smell.

I have found that children who have prepared their own meals are much more likely to try what they have made themselves with a sense of pride and satisfaction. Also unlike other activities this is something boys and girls enjoy equally.

As well as cooking skills there are other areas for child development within food preparation. Children learn mathematical skills whilst calculating and weighing ingredients. They can improve their reading skills reading the recipes, they develop socially by preparing food and proudly sharing with friends and family.

I believe that children experimenting with ingredients from a young age will have the confidence to sit in a restaurant or any dining orientated gathering with ease.

Each recipe in this book is written with child participation in mind. I know the kitchen may seem a scary place for both adults and children, but this book will

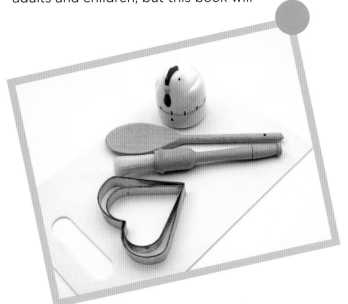

show you how to cook together in a safe, fun environment. Dedicate time – perhaps once a week – by turning the phone and television off, choose a recipe together, have a fun shopping experience and cook! Wear your chef's hats and aprons so that you and the children know this is a serious cooking time.

The key to successful cooking with children is to be prepared. Do all the boring stuff before they come and help you. Have all the ingredients and equipment out. Peel onions and quarter them ready for children to chop safely in the onion chopper.

Don't stress, enjoy the experience, if you drop an egg on the floor don't worry about it just clean it up and get another. When they get flour in their hair remember it just washes out. If your recipe book gets sticky finger prints on it, it's just showing the way it should look, well used.

Read the recipe through thoroughly first and establish to what degree your child can help. Some children will be able to peel and cut a sweet potato for example, whereas others may only manage the peeling and find the chopping too tough, remember the more cooking you do together the more experienced and skilled your children will become.

Remember the kitchen can be a dangerous environment so never take your eyes off the task in hand, give 100% attention and do not get distracted.

So off you go, shop, cook, spend quality time together and above all have some fun.

Be aware and prepare

This section demonstrates how children can safely use different pieces of kitchen equipment supervised and with guidance.

Kitchen Safety
- Minichefs should always have adult supervision.
- Wear an apron to protect your clothing.
- Clear up all mess and spillages as you go, a good chef is a tidy chef.
- There are recipes where very safe plastic knives can be used for younger children. It's better to be taught to use a knife correctly than to be forbidden to use one. When using a knife use a good sawing action for effective cutting. Always keep your fingers behind the blade, right out the way of your fingers.
- Older children will be able to use electric equipment independently under adult supervision. Younger children will require more assistance with electrical equipment.

- Make sure the area and socket are clear from liquids before using electrical equipment. Always make sure your hands are completely dry before using electrical equipment. When using an electric whisk make sure long hair is tied back and the cable is not tangled. Never put your fingers near the blades of the whisk while it's turned on. Keep the whisk on the bottom of the bowl all the time when in use or you will end up with the ingredients sprayed all over yourself, yuck!
- Using plastic coated graters ensures little fingers don't get grated!
- Using vegetable choppers are a safe and fun method of chopping. In preparation an adult can peel and cut an onion into quarters ready for our Minichefs to chop in the chopper. Adults should wash the choppers.
- Using safety peelers correctly prevents accidents. Always place food to be peeled on a chopping board and peel away from your fingers.
- Why buy chopped tomatoes when it's much more fun to squash your own!

Heat Safety

- Always use oven gloves when handling anything hot.
- Always turn cookers off when you have finished cooking.
- Remember cookers are still hot for a while after they have been turned off.

Be Prepared

- Read the recipe through thoroughly before starting to cook.
- Check you have all the ingredients and equipment ready for your recipe.
- Use scales with a clear easy to read gauge. Always make sure the dial is on zero before measuring. The ingredients in this book are measured using grams (g) and centimetres (cm) – metric measurement. Also you will see ounces (oz) and fluid ounces (floz) – imperial measurements. Don't mix the metric with the imperial measurements, stick to one throughout the recipe.

Hygiene

- Scrub nails and wash hands before cooking or handling any food.
- Tie long hair back.
- Don't dip and lick with fingers, use a clean spoon to taste your dish.
- Never dip and lick to taste mixtures with raw egg or flour in them.
- Wash all fruit and vegetables before cooking.
- Always use chopping boards for chopping, never use the work surface.
- Always wash your hands and any equipment after contact with raw meat.
- Make sure all kitchen cloths and teatowels are clean.
- Always store cooked food and raw food separately.
- Raw meat should be stored at the bottom of the fridge and always covered.

Hints and Tips

- When you see the term 'season to taste', it means add a little salt and pepper according to your taste. You should avoid adding salt where possible.
- When a recipe asks you to measure in spoons (teaspoons or tablespoons), it means level spoonfuls rather than heaped. Don't confuse a tablespoon with a dessert spoon, a tablespoon is larger.
- When measuring honey or syrup, warm the required spoon in a mug of hot water first, it will run off the spoon easier.
- To line the bottom with baking paper you draw around the bottom of the dish on paper and cut out. This also stops cakes from sticking.
- The portion sizes in this book are approximate. What may feed a hungry family of four may be enough to feed another family for two days!
- I often use garlic puree in place of fresh garlic, available in jars or tubes from supermarkets. One teaspoon of garlic puree is equivalent to one garlic clove.
- Ginger puree or paste is also used in place of fresh ginger, also in jars or tubes from supermarkets.
- Some recipes in this book require you to core tomatoes. To do this cut a tomato in half through the centre of the core. Make two 'v' shapes cuts around the core to remove.
- When we ask you to 'grease' baking sheets or tins in this book, pour some oil or melted butter into a small bowl and using a pastry brush, lightly brush the sheets with the oil. This stops cakes from sticking.

Breakfast, Lunch & Dinner

Sunrise High Granola Bars

I feel so energetic just looking at the ingredients in these bars!

Makes 12 bars **Preparation** 20 minutes **Oven temperature** 180°C, 350°F, gas mark 4
Cooking time 30 to 35 minutes on the middle shelf
Equipment Scales, Teaspoon, Tablespoon, Pastry brush, a little oil to grease,
baking parchment, 25x18cm (10x7 inch) baking tray, Microwave, 1 large mixing bowl,
1 large mixing spoon, 1 knife

Ingredients

180g (6$\frac{1}{2}$ oz) butter
3 tablespoons clear honey
200g (7oz) Demerara sugar
180g (6$\frac{1}{2}$ oz) rolled oats
120g (4oz) plain flour
1 teaspoon ground cinnamon
50g (2oz) chopped mixed nuts
    (optional)
50g (2oz) sultanas
250g (8oz) dried mixed fruit
    (I like to use pineapple, papaya
    and mango)
50g (2oz) ground almonds (optional)
50g (2oz) chocolate chips
3 tablespoons mixed seeds
50g (2oz) desiccated coconut

Method

1. Pre-heat the oven to 180°C, 350°F, gas mark 4.
   Lightly grease with oil and line the bottom of the
   baking tray with baking paper. In a microwave, melt
   together the butter, honey and sugar. Allow it to
   just come to bubble, about 3 minutes.
2. Stir in all the remaining ingredients and mix really
   well. Press into the prepared baking tray and cook
   for 30 to 35 minutes on the middle shelf of the
   oven until golden in colour. Allow to cool in the tray
   and cut into 12 slices.

Fuelling
your fire,
so you won't tire.

Egg-stra Tasty Toasts

Using brown bread in this eggy bread recipe makes it a much healthier option.

Serves 2 Preparation 15 minutes Cooking time 4 minutes
Equipment Pastry cutters, Small bowl, 1 fork, 1 tablespoon, 1 medium frying pan, Fish slice, Kitchen paper, Teaspoon, Knife, Chopping board

Ingredients

4 slices of thick brown bread
1 egg, lightly beaten in a small bowl
1 tablespoon milk
1 tablespoon golden caster sugar
50g (2oz) butter
1/2 teaspoon ground cinnamon, mixed with 1 tablespoon of golden caster sugar

To serve
a choice of apple, banana, berries, kiwi, orange or dried fruit, crème fraîche

Method

1. Cut shapes out of your four slices of bread. Add the milk and golden caster sugar to the lightly beaten egg and whisk in with a fork.
2. Place the butter into the frying pan and melt over a medium heat. Dip the bread into the egg mixture, hold up to allow any excess to run off and then place carefully into the frying pan. Fry on both sides for about 2 minutes on each side, turning with a fish slice halfway through cooking.
3. When golden and crisp remove from the pan onto kitchen paper. Sprinkle each toast with cinnamon and the caster sugar mixture. Serve with slices of fresh fruit, apple, banana, berries, orange or any dried fruit and a dollop of crème fraîche.

Dairy Fruity Oat Floats

Prepare this delicious dish before you go to bed ready for a healthy start the next morning.

Serves 2 Preparation 15 minutes Refrigeration overnight
Equipment 1 large mixing bowl, Scales, Tablespoon, 1 knife,
Chopping board, 1 large mixing spoon, Measuring jug

Ingredients

Option 1

150g (5oz) porridge oats
200g (7oz) apricot yoghurt
75ml (2floz) milk
a handful of dried apricots, sliced
150ml (5floz) milk for the next morning
1 banana, peeled and sliced
a handful of pecan nuts
1 tablespoon runny honey

Option 2

150g (5oz) porridge oats
200g (7oz) strawberry yoghurt
75ml (2floz) milk
150ml (5floz) milk for the next morning
a handful of sliced strawberries
1 tablespoon strawberry jam mixed
with 1 tablespoon boiling water to
make jam sauce

Method

Option 1

1. Pour the oats, apricot yoghurt, milk and apricots in a large bowl and mix together well. Cover with cling film and leave in the fridge overnight.
2. The next morning mix in the extra milk, pour the mixture between 2 serving bowls and top with sliced banana, pecan nuts and drizzle with honey.

Option 2

1. Pour the oats, strawberry yoghurt and milk in a large bowl and mix together well. Cover with cling film and leave in the fridge overnight.
2. The next morning mix in the extra milk, pour the mixture between 2 serving bowls and top with sliced strawberries and drizzle with jam sauce.

Taj Ma-Dhal

Tarka dhal is a traditional Indian vegetarian dish served with rice or as a side dish served with other Indian delights.

This recipe is a great way of showing how we get a delicious curry flavour by mixing different Indian spices together rather than just using curry powder. Red split lentils contain a high carbohydrate count and contain several vitamins and minerals.

Makes 2 large portions, 4 small side portions Preparation 20 minutes
Cooking time 20 minutes
Equipment 2 saucepans, Tablespoon, Teaspoon, Knife, Sieve, Large spoon, Chopping board, Onion chopper

Ingredients

200g (7oz) red split lentils, rinsed in
    cold water
500ml (18floz) boiling water
2 tablespoons sunflower oil
1 onion, finely chopped (an adult
    can peel and 1/4 the onion ready
    for chopping)
1 teaspoon cumin seeds
1 teaspoon ginger puree
1 teaspoon garlic puree
1/2 teaspoon chilli powder
1/2 teaspoon garam masala
1/2 teaspoon ground fenugreek
1 tablespoon tomato puree
3 fat juicy tomatoes, cored and cut
    into small dice
1 handful of chopped fresh coriander
seasoning to taste
rice to serve

Method

1. Cook the lentils in the boiling water gently for about 15 minutes, rinse in a sieve with cold water.
2. In another pan heat the sunflower oil. Add the onion, cumin seeds, ginger, garlic, chilli, garam masala, and fenugreek and cook stirring over a medium heat for 2 to 3 minutes.
3. Add the tomato puree and diced tomatoes and cook for another 2 to 3 minutes, season to taste.
4. Add the cooked lentils, gently heat through and stir in the coriander. Serve straight away and enjoy.

Minced Moo Madras

Here's a tasty, perhaps English, twist for a curry dish.

Serves 4 portions Preparation 15 minutes Cooking time 30 minutes
Equipment Tablespoon, Onion chopper, Large saucepan, Teaspoon, Large spoon, Measuring jug

Ingredients

1 tablespoon sunflower oil

1 onion, finely chopped (an adult can peel and 1/4 the onion ready for chopping)

1 teaspoon garlic puree

1 teaspoon ginger puree

1 teaspoon ground cumin

1 teaspoon ground coriander

1 or 2 tablespoons mild or medium curry powder to taste

500g (16oz) lean minced beef

1 beef stock cube dissolved in 200ml (7floz) of water

400g (14oz) chopped tinned tomatoes (or squash plum tomatoes with your fingers)

1 bay leaf

1 tablespoon mango chutney

200g (7oz) frozen petits pois

salt and pepper

basmati rice to serve

Method

1. Heat the oil in a large saucepan and add the onion, garlic, ginger, cumin, coriander, curry powder and beef. Brown all the ingredients stirring continuously over a medium heat for about five minutes.

2. Add the stock and tomatoes, bay leaf and mango chutney and season to taste. Bring to the boil and then reduce the heat to simmer for about 30 minutes.

3. Add the petit pois and cook for a further 5 minutes. Serve on a bed of basmati rice.

Spicy Pasties
You could use this spicy mince to make tasty little pasties in short crust or puff pastry baked in the oven.

Squashed Piggy Curry

Pork, butternut squash and sweet potato curry

This is a great way of introducing butternut squash and sweet potato into a child's diet. By grating the squash and sweet potato the vegetables disappear into a nice smooth sauce, sometimes more appealing to young taste buds than chunks of vegetables.

Serves 4 portions Cooking time 45 minutes Preparation 20 minutes
Equipment Chopping board, Peeler, Grater, Onion chopper, Knife, Large saucepan, Teaspoon, Measuring jug, Large spoon, Tablespoon

Ingredients

1 tablespoon sunflower oil

1 large onion, finely chopped (an adult can peel and 1/4 the onion ready for chopping)

500g (16oz) diced pork loin, fat removed (cut into 2cm cubes)

1 teaspoon garlic puree

1 small butternut squash, about 250g (8oz) peeled, seeded and grated

1 medium sweet potato, about 500g (16oz) peeled and grated

1 or 2 tablespoons mild or medium curry powder

1 teaspoon turmeric

1 teaspoon ground coriander

1 teaspoon ground cumin

1 teaspoon ginger puree

1 vegetable stock cube dissolved in 700ml (24floz) hot water

1 bay leaf

3 tablespoons crème fraîche

salt and pepper

Method

1. Heat the oil in a large pan and fry the onion and pork until sealed and starting to brown, about 5 minutes.
2. Add the garlic, squash, sweet potato, curry powder, turmeric, coriander, cumin and ginger and fry for a further 2 minutes.
3. Add the vegetable stock and bay leaf. Bring to the boil then simmer covered for about 45 minutes to 1 hour until the pork is nice and tender. Season to taste.
4. Before serving stir in 3 tablespoons of crème fraîche. Serve on a bed of rice.

This is a seriously tasty curry dish!

Tasty Taj Triangles

Tasty little Indian-style vegetable samosas are a great lunchtime, lunch box or party snack. You don't need to pre-cook the vegetables in the recipe, defrosting and oven baking is sufficient.

Makes 12 samosas   Cooking time 20 minutes   Oven temperature 220°C, 425°F, gas mark 7
Preparation 20 minutes
Equipment Scales, Large mixing bowl, Tablespoon, Knife, Pastry brush, Baking sheet, Large spoon

Ingredients

200g (7oz) mixed frozen vegetables, defrosted

1 tablespoon mild or medium curry powder

2 tablespoons mango chutney

100g (3½ oz) white or brown long grain rice or basmati rice, cooked according to packet instructions

salt and pepper

270g (9oz) packet filo pastry (6 sheets)

2 tablespoons sunflower oil

Method

1. Preheat the oven to 220°C, 425°F, gas mark 7. In a mixing bowl mix together all the ingredients except the pastry and oil. Season to taste.

2. Place a sheet of filo pastry onto a work surface. Cut in half lengthways to give 2 strips of pastry 12cm by 47cm. Place 2 tablespoons of rice mixture near the top left corner of each strip. Fold the corner over the rice to make a triangle. Fold the triangle down and continue to fold down, to keep the triangle shape until all the pastry is used.

3. Repeat to make 12 parcels. Place on a greased baking sheet, brush all over with oil and bake in the pre-heated oven for about 20 minutes, until golden brown. Enjoy.

However
you eat them,
whenever you
eat them, you are sure
to enjoy them!

Cluck Tuck

These bread-crumbed turkey/chicken nuggets with a creamy cranberry dip are a great alternative to roast turkey at Christmas or chicken anytime of the year. You could also serve these crispy nuggets at a party as finger food.

Makes 18 large nuggets **Preparation** 20 minutes
Oven temperature 200°C, 400°F, gas mark 6 **Cooking time** 15 to 20 minutes
Equipment Baking sheet, Pastry brush, Chopping board, Knife, 3 shallow bowls, Rolling pin, Sandwich bag, Fork, Tablespoon

Ingredients

500g (16oz) boneless, skinless turkey or chicken breast
100g (3^1/$_2$ oz) crushed cornflakes
2 eggs, lightly beaten, mixed with 2 tablespoons milk
salt and pepper
6 tablespoons plain flour
2 tablespoons grated parmesan cheese
3 slices of medium white or brown bread made into breadcrumbs
2 tablespoons sunflower oil

For the creamy cranberry dip
2 tablespoons mayonnaise mixed with 1 tablespoon cranberry sauce or jelly

Method

1. Pre-heat the oven to 200°C, 400°F, gas mark 6. Using a pastry brush lightly grease a baking sheet with a little sunflower oil. Cut the turkey or chicken breasts into 10x3cm (4x1inch) strips.
2. Place the cornflakes in a sandwich bag, twist the top of the bag expelling all the air, and bash with the rolling pin. MIND YOUR FINGERS!
3. Place the egg and milk mixture into a shallow bowl and season to taste with salt and pepper. In another bowl place the flour and in the last bowl mix together the crushed cornflakes, parmesan cheese and breadcrumbs.
4. Dip the chicken or turkey, one by one, first into the flour then into the egg and milk and finally into the crushed cornflakes mixture. Repeat this with all the meat strips until all have been coated.
5. Place on the greased baking sheet and bake in the pre-heated oven for 15 to 20 minutes until crisp and golden. Serve with cranberry dip and enjoy.

Fishy Wishy On A Dishy

Move over fish fingers. These salmon and potato fish cakes are tasty, healthy and great fun to make. Get fishing kids. An adult may need to cut the raw potatoes into chunks as they are quite tough to cut.

Makes 4 fish cakes **Preparation** 25 minutes **Oven temperature** 200°C, 400°F, gas mark 6
Cooking time 20 minutes
Equipment Baking sheet, Pastry brush, Chopping board, Knife, Fork, 3 shallow bowls, Potato masher, Large spoon to mix, Tablespoon, Large bowl, Peeler, Large saucepan

Ingredients

400g (13oz) salmon fillets

25g (1oz) butter

400g (13oz) potatoes peeled, cut into chunks and cooked until soft

1 tablespoon milk

2 spring onions, finely chopped

salt and pepper

100g (3 1/2 oz) plain flour

2 eggs beaten lightly, mixed with 2 tablespoons of milk, seasoned

5 slices of medium white or brown bread made into breadcrumbs using a food processor and mixed with 40g (1 1/2 oz) sesame seeds

salt and pepper

To serve

Frozen peas cooked according to packet instructions

Lemon wedges

Method

1. Pre-heat the oven to 200°C, 400°F, gas mark 6. Place the salmon fillets onto a greased baking sheet. Put some small knobs of butter over the top and bake in the pre-heated oven for 15 to 20 minutes and allow to cool, remove the skins.

2. Place the cooked potatoes in a large bowl and mash with the butter and milk.

3. Add the salmon, spring onions, salt and pepper. Mix well.

4. Dust your hands with flour and divide the salmon mixture into 4 equal balls. Flatten slightly.

5. Place the flour, egg and milk mixture, and breadcrumbs into separate shallow bowls. Coat the fishcakes first in flour, then the egg and milk and finally the breadcrumbs. Mould them into fish shapes by pressing down on the mixture and pinching one end to resemble a tail.

6. Place on a greased baking sheet and cook in the pre-heated oven for about 20 minutes until crisp and golden.

Tartar sauce

Ingredients

6 tablespoons mayonnaise
1 tablespoon capers, chopped
1 tablespoon chopped fresh parsley
2 tablespoons chopped gherkins

Method

1. To make the tartar sauce just mix all the ingredients together.

Serve fish cakes decorated with cooked peas, lemon and homemade tartar sauce.

Burgers To Relish

Preparation 15 minutes Makes 4 burgers
Oven temperature 200°C, 400°F, gas mark 6
Cooking time 20 minutes
Equipment Large mixing bowl, Large spoon, Onion chopper,
Tablespoon, Teaspoon, Knife, Chopping board, Baking sheet

**Serve with
Wacky Wedges
and enjoy.**

Claire Mc's

Beef burgers with a secret cheese centre.

Ingredients

500g (16oz) lean minced beef
1 medium onion finely chopped
**(an adult can peel and 1/4 the onion
ready for chopping)**
2 tablespoons dried mixed herbs
1 tablespoon fresh chopped parsley
1 teaspoon garlic puree
1 tablespoon tomato ketchup
1 egg yolk
salt and pepper
**50g (2oz) Cheddar cheese cut into
4 cubes**

Method

1. Pre-heat the oven to 200°C, 400°F, gas mark 6
   and lightly grease a baking sheet. Place all of the
   ingredients except the cheese into a large mixing
   bowl and mix together well.
2. Divide the mixture into 4 and mould into burger
   shapes. Place a cube of cheese into the centre of
   each burger and cover with meat. Place onto
   prepared baking sheet.
3. Bake in the pre-heated oven for about 20 minutes
   until thoroughly cooked. Serve in burger buns with
   your choice of lettuce, mayonnaise, ketchup and
   tomatoes.
4. Serve with Wacky Wedges (page 30).

Bombay Burgers

A mild curried burger.

Ingredients

500g (16oz) lean minced beef
1 medium onion, finely chopped
1 tablespoon chopped fresh parsley
1 teaspoon garlic puree
2 tablespoons mild or medium
**   curry powder**
2 tablespoons mango chutney
1 egg yolk
salt and pepper

Method

1. Pre-heat the oven to 200°C, 400°F, gas mark 6 and lightly grease a baking sheet. Place all of the ingredients into a large mixing bowl and mix together well.
2. Divide the mixture into 4 and mould into burger shapes and place onto the prepared baking sheet.
3. Bake in the pre-heated oven for about 20 minutes until thoroughly cooked. Serve in burger buns with your choice of lettuce, mayonnaise, ketchup and tomatoes.

Wacky Wedges

Make your own potato wedges – plain or spicy. Wacky wedges are a wonderful tasty alternative to chips or French fries. An adult may need to cut up the tough potatoes into wedges.

Serves with 4 burgers Preparation 10 minutes Oven temperature 200°C, 400°F, gas mark 6
Cooking time 40 minutes
Equipment Serrated knife, Tablespoon, Teaspoon, Baking sheet

Ingredients

2 medium sweet potatoes cut into thin wedges, skins left on

2 jacket potatoes cut into wedges, skins left on

2 tablespoons olive oil

2 teaspoons Spanish paprika

Method

1. Pre-heat the oven to 200°C, 400°F, gas mark 6. Toss all of the ingredients together in a large bowl and place onto a greased baking sheet. Season to taste.

2. Bake in the oven for 30 to 40 minutes until soft in the centre and golden and crispy on the outside.

Curry Curunchies

For wedges with a kick replace the paprika with curry powder and follow the same instructions.

King Of Ketchups

Why not make your own tomato ketchup for the recipes in this section.

Preparation 15 minutes **Cooking time** 45 minutes
Equipment Onion chopper, Large saucepan, Teaspoon, Knife, Tablespoon, Chopping board

It's a great
way of
using up over ripe
tomatoes.

Ingredients
1 tablespoon sunflower oil
1 teaspoon garlic puree
1 onion, finely chopped (an adult
 can peel and 1/4 the onion ready
 for chopping)
12 really ripe tomatoes, cut into small
 dice with the core removed
1 tablespoon vinegar
1 teaspoon soft brown sugar
salt and pepper to taste

Method
1. Heat the oil in a pan and cook the garlic puree and onion until soft, about 5 minutes.
2. Add the tomatoes, vinegar and sugar and bring to the boil. Reduce the heat and simmer for about 45 minutes. If it appears to be drying out whilst cooking add some water.
3. Blend in a liquidiser. This will keep in the fridge in an airtight container or bottle for about 2 weeks.

Porky Pasta

Why buy the more expensive tinned chopped tomatoes for this pasta and sausage dish when you can buy plum tomatoes, pop them in a jug and squash them with your hands? Fun, fun, fun!

Serves 4 Cooking time 35 minutes Preparation 20 minutes
Equipment Large saucepan, Large spoon, Onion chopper, Chopping board, Grater, Peeler, Teaspoon, Measuring jug, Tablespoon, Knife

Ingredients

200g (7oz) pasta shapes, cooked
    according to packet instructions
1 tablespoon olive oil
1 onion, finely chopped (an adult can
    peel and 1/4 the onion ready for
    chopping)
2 carrots, peeled and grated
1 teaspoon garlic puree
200g (7oz) sausage meat
400g tin chopped tomatoes
1 vegetable stock cube, dissolved
    in 200ml (7floz) of water
1 bay leaf
1 teaspoon dried oregano
1 handful freshly torn basil leaves
    and a little extra to sprinkle over
    the finished dish
100g (3 1/2 oz) grated cheese (I like to
    use mozzarella for this recipe)
salt and pepper

Method

1. Heat the olive oil in a large saucepan over a medium heat. Add the onion, carrots, garlic and sausage meat. Cook stirring continuously breaking up the sausage meat with a spoon for 5 minutes until starting to brown.
2. Add the tomatoes, stock, bay leaf and oregano, bring to the boil and reduce to simmer for 30 minutes.
3. After 30 minutes season to taste, stir in the pasta and basil and serve sprinkled with grated cheese and freshly torn basil leaves. Enjoy.

Pizza The Action

These puff pastry pizzas are so quick to make. This is the simple cheese and tomato version but you can add mushrooms, peppers, meat, pineapple, onion or any other topping you fancy.

Makes 4 pizzas **Preparation** 15 minutes **Cooking time** 15 to 20 minutes
Oven temperature 200°C, 400°F, gas mark 6
Equipment Rolling pin, Bowl, Tablespoon, Baking trays, Knife, Teaspoon

Ingredients

flour to dust

250g (8oz, 1/2 a packet) ready roll puff pastry

8 tablespoons passata

1 teaspoon garlic puree

1 handful of torn fresh basil leaves and a little extra to serve

125g (4oz) ball of mozzarella, cut into thin slices

2 tomatoes, sliced

salt and pepper

Method

1. Pre-heat the oven to 200°C, 400°F, gas mark 6. Lightly flour the work surface. Gently roll out the pastry to a 30 x 40cm (12 x 16inch) rectangle. Cut into 4. Flour your fingers and pinch the pastry around the edges. Place on the baking trays.

2. In a bowl mix together the passata, garlic puree and basil. Season to taste. Spoon over the pastry rectangles leaving a few centimetres from the edge. Arrange the sliced mozzarella and tomatoes over the top.

3. Bake in the pre-heated oven for 15 to 20 minutes, until golden and risen. Serve hot or cold with a sprinkling of freshly torn basil leaves. Enjoy.

Dough Balls

The smell of these garlic and herb dough balls cooking will make your mouth water. Serve with all kinds of Italian dishes.

Makes 12 dough balls **Preparation** 15 minutes **Oven temperature** 180°C, 350°F, gas mark 4
Cooking time 20 minutes
Equipment Large bowl, Electric whisk, Teaspoon, Measuring jug, Grater, Muffin tray, Tablespoons

Ingredients

200g (7oz) self-raising flour
1 teaspoon baking powder
1/2 teaspoon salt
100g (3 1/2 oz) butter, at room
**   temperature**
2 teaspoons sugar
1 egg
150 ml (5floz) milk
2 teaspoons garlic puree
100g (3 1/2 oz) grated cheddar cheese
2 teaspoons dried basil
grated Parmesan to sprinkle

Method

1. Pre-heat the oven to 180°C, 350°F, gas mark 4. Line a 12 section muffin tray with paper cases. Place all of the ingredients except the Parmesan cheese into a large bowl. Whisk together using an electric whisk until light and fluffy.
2. Spoon the mixture into the prepared muffin tray. Sprinkle with grated Parmesan. Bake in the pre-heated oven for 20 minutes until golden and risen. Enjoy with soup or pasta dishes.

Gourd-geous Risotto

I love this tasty supper dish of butternut squash in a traditional rice risotto. Served by itself, it is a wholesome, substantial healthy choice. Rice is a carbohydrate food, suitable for those with gluten or wheat intolerance. Butternut squash is a member of the gourd family, a winter squash you could substitute with pumpkin.

Serves 4 medium portions Preparation 20 minutes Cooking time 30 minutes
Equipment Large saucepan, Measuring jug, Knife, Chopping board, Grater, Scales, Measuring jug, Large spoon, Teaspoon

Ingredients

50g (2oz) butter
1 leek, finely sliced and washed
100g (3^1/$_2$ oz) smoked ham or bacon, sliced
1 butternut squash about 500g (16oz) peeled, de-seeded and grated
1 teaspoon garlic puree
300g (10oz) Arborio rice
2 vegetable stock cubes, dissolved in 1.2 litres (2 pints) of hot water
100g (3^1/$_2$ oz) grated Parmesan cheese to serve
salt and pepper
a little chopped fresh parsley

Method

1. Heat the butter in a large saucepan. Add the leek, bacon, squash and garlic puree and fry, stirring continuously for about 7 minutes.
2. Add the rice and half of the vegetable stock and stir well. Cook simmering until all the stock has been absorbed, about 5 minutes.
3. Add the remaining stock and cook, simmering, and stirring occasionally for about 15 minutes, the stock will have been absorbed, the rice will be cooked and creamy. Season to taste. Serve sprinkled with grated Parmesan cheese and a little chopped fresh parsley.

NOTE Young Minichefs may find it difficult to peel and cut the sweet potato and butternut squash ready for grating. You can leave that to the grown ups and leave the grating to the strong arm of our Minichefs!

Chick Sticks

Each recipe makes 4 large kebabs

Here (and on page 40) are three tasty, colourful chicken kebab recipes. Serve them with the coconut rice or funky yellow rice. You could pack them cold for picnics or lunchboxes or pop them onto the barbecue.

Preparation 20 minutes plus at least 2 hours refrigeration
Cooking time 20 minutes **Oven temperature** 220°C, 425°F, gas mark 7
Equipment Chopping board, Knife, Saucepan for peanut sauce, 4 wooden skewers, Bowl for marinade, Tablespoon, Teaspoon, Baking sheet, Spoon for mixing

Ingredients

For all Chick Sticks

500g (16oz) boneless, skinless chicken breast, cut into large cubes
1 medium onion, peeled and cut into 8
1 small pepper, any colour, de-seeded and cubed into about 8 pieces
4 long wooden kebab skewers

Marinade 1
Sticky Chicken

4 tablespoons clear honey
2 tablespoons Worcestershire sauce
8 tablespoons tomato ketchup
1 tablespoon whole grain mustard
1 teaspoon garlic puree
1 tablespoon lemon juice

Method

1. This method is to be used for all the Chick Sticks. Mix all of the marinade ingredients together in a large bowl with the diced chicken. Cover with cling film and marinade in the fridge for at least 2 hours. I prefer to leave them in over night for a fuller flavour. Soak the wooden kebab skewers in water for about 1 hour, this prevents them splitting or burning in the oven.

2. Pre-heat the oven to 220°C, 425°F, gas mark 7. Place the cubes of chicken on the skewers alternating with the onion and pepper (and pineapple for peanutty chicken) until all have been used up.

3. Place on a greased baking sheet and pour over any remaining marinade, bake in the oven for 20 minutes, turning once through cooking and spooning the juices over the top. Serve with Funky Yellow Rice and salad or Coconut Rice and Beans.

Marinade 2
Sticky Marmalade Chicken

4 tablespoons fine cut marmalade, microwaved for about 1 minute

4 tablespoons light soy sauce

1 teaspoon fresh or dried thyme

1 tablespoon olive oil

a few fresh orange wedges to serve with the cooked kebabs

Marinade 3
Peanutty Chicks Sticks

1 tablespoon sweet chilli sauce

1 teaspoon garlic puree

4 tablespoons light soy sauce

1 tablespoon lemon juice

1 teaspoon ground cumin

1 teaspoon ground coriander

1 teaspoon ground turmeric

1 teaspoon soft brown sugar

227g (1 small tin) pineapple chunks to add to the skewers with the chicken

peppers and onion

Peanutty Sauce

Ingredients

200ml tin coconut milk

6 tablespoons crunchy peanut butter

1 tablespoon soy sauce

1 teaspoon soft brown sugar

1 teaspoon garlic puree

Method

1. To make the peanut sauce pour all the ingredients into a saucepan stirring until smooth and bubbling. Serve on side of Peanutty Chick Sticks.

Equipment for Rice dishes Sieve for rinsing and straining, Large saucepan, Large spoon to stir and serve, Tin opener

Colourful tasty rice to go with your kebabs

Funky Yellow Rice

Ingredients
allow 75g (3oz) of rice per person or 300g (10oz) for 4 people
1 tablespoon turmeric

Method
1. Rinse the rice in cold water before cooking.
2. Cook according to the packet instructions adding 1 tablespoon of turmeric to the boiling water.

Coconut Rice And Beans

Ingredients
allow 75g (3oz) basmati rice per person or 300g (10oz) for 4 people
200ml coconut milk
200g (1 small tin) kidney beans, drained

Method
1. Cook the rice according to the packet instructions, drain and rinse with cold water.
2. Put the coconut milk into a saucepan and bring to the boil. Stir in the rice, reduce the heat and stir continuously until all the coconut milk has been absorbed. Finally stir in the kidney beans.

Eggsplosion!

A sausage, mash and beans volcano! This is a really original way to serve a classic and much loved combination. An adult may need to cut the raw potatoes into chunks; they are quite tough to cut.

Serves 2 Preparation 25 minutes Cooking time 5 minutes
Equipment Peeler, Knife, 2 saucepans, Strainer, Masher, Large spoon, Blunt knife, Frying pan, Fish slice, Chopping board

Ingredients

For the mash
900g (30oz) potatoes peeled
100g (3¹/2 oz) butter
150ml (5floz) full fat milk
2 spring onions, topped, tailed and
    finely sliced
salt and pepper

For the volcano
4 best quality sausages, cooked
400g tin baked beans
2 tablespoons sunflower oil
2 eggs

Method

1. Cut the potatoes into equal sizes. Bring a pan of salted water to the boil and add the potatoes. Boil for about 15 minutes or until soft. Drain the potatoes; put them back into the saucepan. Add the butter and milk, salt and pepper and mash until smooth, stir in the spring onions. Heat the baked beans.

2. Divide the mash between 2 plates and use a blunt knife to make into a cone shape with a flat top. Cut the cooked sausages in half, lengthways and widthways and place up the sides of the potato. You want your sausages to be hot, but not too hot to handle! Place the baked beans around the bottom of the mountain.

3. Finally heat the oil in a frying pan and fry the eggs and place at the top of the volcano and break the yolk; it will look like lava running down the side of your mountain.

Bangers & Bean Bowls

Sausage, potato and baked bean stew. An adult may need to cut the raw potatoes, carrots and parsnips into chunks; they are quite tough to cut.

Serves 4 Preparation 20 minutes Cooking time 25 minutes
Equipment Tablespoon, Onion chopper, Knife, Peeler, Measuring jug, Large saucepan, Tin opener, Teaspoon

Ingredients

1 tablespoon sunflower oil

1 onion, finely chopped (an adult can peel and 1/4 the onion ready for chopping)

4 medium potatoes, peeled and cut into small chunks

2 medium parsnips, peeled and cut into small chunks

2 medium carrots, peeled and cut into small chunks

400ml (14floz) water

1 vegetable stock cube

1 bay leaf

400g tin chopped tomatoes

1 tablespoon Worcestershire sauce

1/2 teaspoon English mustard powder

400g tin baked beans

8 best quality sausages, cooked and cut into chunks (or 4 cooked chicken breasts sliced)

Method

1. Heat the oil in a large pan; add the onion, potatoes, parsnips and carrots. Fry stirring for about 5 minutes until the vegetables start to brown.
2. In a jug mix together the water, stock cube, bay leaf, tomatoes, Worcestershire sauce and mustard powder, add to the vegetables and simmer for about 20 minutes until the vegetables are cooked.
3. Add the beans and sausages to the pan, heat through, serve and enjoy.

Chick Pea and Spanish Sausage Stew

Whilst on my travels in Spain I was introduced to a family who run a tapas bar in the small mountain village called Sedella. I couldn't resist the opportunity to have a tapas cookery lesson with Neil and his granddaughter Cara. We had enormous fun and I hope you'll agree the result is delicious. This is a Spanish dish loved by all, called Garbanzos y Chorizos. It's healthy, filling and satisfying and using the freshest and best chorizo helps.

Serves 4 Preparation 20 minutes Cooking time 20 minutes
Equipment Chopping board, Knife, Onion chopper, Large saucepan, Tablespoon, Teaspoon

Ingredients

2 tablespoons olive oil
2 medium onions, finely chopped (an
　　adult can peel and 1/4 the onion
　　ready for chopping)
1 teaspoon garlic puree
400g (13oz) chorizo, chopped into
　　chunks
690g (23oz) passata, sieved tomatoes
1/2 teaspoon cayenne pepper
400g tin chickpeas
salt and freshly ground pepper

Method

1. Heat the oil in a large saucepan and fry the onions for about 5 minutes, until they start to brown, then add the garlic and the chorizo. Fry slowly over a low heat for around 5 minutes and stir occasionally.
2. Stir in the passata and cayenne and simmer over a low heat for about 10 minutes.
3. Now add the drained chickpeas and heat through. Season to taste, serve with chunks of fresh crusty bread.

This is a Spanish dish loved by all, called Garbanzos y Chorizos.

My Daddy's Irish Stew

My Dad was from Belfast and this stew is a McAvoy family tradition. It was the only thing he ever cooked! I used to love it so much I would dive into the middle and burn my mouth and he would always say "round the edges" which is always cooler. I always have mine with brown sauce. You can use frozen vegetables for this recipe, just as my Dad did, but I do prefer to use fresh vegetables. An adult may need to cut the raw potatoes, swede, carrots and parsnips into chunks; they are quite tough to cut.

Serves 6 to 8 portions Preparation 30 minutes Cooking time 30 to 40 minutes
Equipment Knife, Chopping board, Onion chopper, Peeler, Tablespoon,
Large thick bottomed saucepan, Large spoon, Potato masher

Ingredients

1 tablespoon sunflower oil

1 large onion, peeled and finely chopped (an adult can peel and $1/4$ the onion ready for chopping)

500g (16oz) very lean minced beef

1 medium swede, about 500g (16oz), peeled and roughly chopped

4 medium carrots, about 300g (10oz), peeled and roughly chopped

2 medium parsnips, about 300g (10oz), peeled and roughly chopped

2 medium leeks, about 200g (7oz), washed and sliced

2 sticks of celery, washed and sliced

6 medium potatoes, peeled and cut into chunks, about 1kg (32oz)

2 beef stock cubes dissolved in 1.2 litres (2 pints) of water

Method

1. Heat the oil in a large saucepan, add the onion and mince and cook for 5 minutes stirring continuously and breaking up the mince with a large spoon.

2. Add the vegetables and cook stirring for another 5 minutes.

3. Cover with stock, add the potatoes, bring to the boil and reduce to a gentle simmer. All the meat and vegetables should be just covered, if not add a bit more water. Simmer gently for 30 to 40 minutes until all the vegetables are very tender and ready to mash.

4. Using a potato masher, mash all the ingredients together. Season to taste and serve

This has no resemblance what-so-ever to a real Irish stew!

Couscous & Pepper Traffic De-lights

Couscous is fine grains of semolina. Most couscous has been pre-cooked and just requires soaking in order to reconstitute it.

Serves 3 large portions or 6 small portions Preparation 35 minutes including making the sauce Cooking time peppers 20 minutes, sauce 15 minutes
Oven temperature 220°C, 425°F, gas mark 7
Equipment Saucepan, 1 measuring jug, Serrated knife, Grater, Chopping board, Pastry brush, Baking sheet

Ingredients

200ml (7floz) boiling water
   with one vegetable stock cube
   crumbled into it
100g (3¹/₂ oz) couscous
1 red pepper
1 yellow pepper
1 green pepper
2 large ripe tomatoes, cut into small
   dice, removing the core
50g (2oz) smoked ham, fat removed
   and thinly sliced
a small handful of freshly torn basil
   leaves
2 spring onions, topped and tailed
   and finely sliced
50g (2oz) grated cheese
olive oil for brushing

Method

1. Pre-heat the oven to 220°C, 425°F, gas mark 7. In a saucepan bring the stock to the boil, add the couscous and stir well. Remove the saucepan from the heat and cover with a lid and leave to stand until all the water is just about absorbed, about 3 minutes.

2. Halve the 3 peppers leaving the cores in place and scoop out the seeds. Brush them all over with olive oil, season to taste, and bake in the oven for 10 minutes.

3. Meanwhile, add the diced tomatoes, sliced ham, basil and spring onions to the couscous and stir well.

4. When the peppers have cooked for 10 minutes remove them from the oven, fill them with the couscous mixture and sprinkle with grated cheese. Return to the hot oven and cook for 10 minutes. Serve with some tomato sauce.

Tomato Sauce

Ingredients

1 tablespoon olive oil
1 teaspoon garlic puree
400g tin chopped tomatoes
a small handful of freshly torn basil leaves
1 teaspoon sugar
salt and pepper

Method

1. Heat the oil in a saucepan and add the garlic. Stir for 2 minutes.
2. Add the chopped tomatoes, basil and sugar and allow it to simmer for 15 minutes.
3. Add salt and pepper and serve with the stuffed peppers.

Try these brightly coloured peppers filled with couscous for a tasty healthy supper dish.

Bonkers
About
Baking

Roll Up For Bananas

Filo, banana and maple rolls

They freeze really well and can be re-heated from frozen or thawed. They are delicious served with coconut ice cream or custard.

Makes 16 rolls Preparation 25 minutes Cooking time 15 to 20 minutes
Oven temperature 200°C, 400°F, gas mark 6
Equipment Knife, Large bowl, Tablespoon, Small bowl, Large spoon, Pastry brush, Baking sheet

Ingredients

270g (9oz) packet or 6 sheets filo pastry (if frozen, defrost first)
4 small ripe bananas peeled
2 tablespoons lemon juice
4 tablespoons maple flavour golden syrup
100g (3¹/₂oz) melted butter

These little banana parcels are a delicious crisp dessert.

Method

1. Pre-heat the oven to 200°C, 400°F, gas mark 6. Cut the bananas in half lengthways, then each of these pieces in half again down the middle.
2. Put the lemon juice and maple flavour golden syrup in a large bowl and gently toss the bananas in it.
3. Lay the filo pastry on a work surface. It will have 6 layers. Split in half so you have 2 rectangles of pastry, 3 layers deep. Brush both with melted butter.
4. Cut each rectangle into 8 even squares. Place a piece of banana into the centre of a square, fold in the 2 sides and roll up around the banana. Repeat this with all the banana and pastry pieces. Don't throw away the remaining lemon and maple mixture.
5. Brush all over with butter and place on a greased baking sheet. Brush the tops with the remaining lemon and maple mixture. Bake in the oven for about 15 to 20 minutes until golden and crispy. Serve pouring any reaming lemon and maple mixture over the top and serve with coconut ice cream.

Cheesey, Chivey Scones

Serve these delicious scones warm with butter, cream cheese, thinly sliced ham or just anything you fancy....yum!

Makes 5 or 6 scones Preparation 15 minutes Oven temperature 200°C, 400°F, gas mark 6
Cooking time 10 to 15 minutes
Equipment Baking sheet, Sieve, Knife, Large bowl, Teaspoon, Measuring jug,
3 inch pastry cutter, Rolling pin, Tablespoon, Scales

Ingredients

120g (4oz) wholemeal flour

120g (4oz) self-raising flour

1 level teaspoon baking powder

a pinch of salt

60g (2¹/₂ oz) butter, cut into knobs at
    room temperature

¹/₂ teaspoon English mustard powder

1 tablespoon snipped fresh chives

100g (3¹/₂ oz) mature cheddar, grated

125ml (4floz) milk

paprika to sprinkle

60g (2¹/₂ oz) pine nuts (optional)

Method

1. Pre-heat the oven to 200°C, 400°F, gas mark 6. Lightly grease a baking sheet. Sift the flours into a large bowl. Add the baking powder and salt. Add the butter and using your fingertips rub together until the mixture resembles fine breadcrumbs.

2. Stir in the mustard, chives, cheese and enough milk to bring the ingredients together to form soft dough.

3. Roll the dough on a floured work surface to a 2.5 cm (1inch) thickness. Using a 7 or 8cm (3inch) cutter cut out the scones. Repeat until all the dough has been used.

4. Place the scones on the baking sheet, brush with milk and sprinkle with the pine nuts (if using) and paprika. Gently press the pine nuts into the scones. Bake for 10 to 15 minutes until golden and risen. Enjoy.

Yum!

Blarney Bread

This is one of Max's mum's recipes she has shared with us. This bread takes me back to my childhood when wheaten bread would be served with a big Ulster fry up mmmm! For a healthier choice you can make fresh sandwiches with it or you could have it warm with butter and cream cheese. Whatever your choice it's delicious, thanks Janine.

Makes 1 round loaf (17cm, 7inches) Oven temperature 200°C, 400°F, gas mark 6
Preparation 15 minutes Cooking time 20 to 25 minutes
Equipment Baking sheet, Large bowl, Tablespoon, Teaspoon, Scales, Brush for greasing, Knife

Ingredients

150g (5oz) wholemeal flour or granary malted brown bread flour

50g (2oz) plain flour

1 teaspoon bicarbonate of soda

1 teaspoon salt

25g (1oz) butter

1 tablespoon golden syrup

150ml (5floz) buttermilk (1/2 a carton)

Method

1. Pre-heat the oven to 200°C, 400°F, gas mark 6. Lightly grease a baking sheet. Sieve the flours into a mixing bowl and tip any grains left over back into the bowl. Add the bicarbonate of soda and salt. Using your finger tips rub the butter into the flour until it resembles fine breadcrumbs.

2. Add the golden syrup, and buttermilk and mix to form a soft dough. Mould into a round loaf, about 17cm (7inches) in diameter, cut a cross into the top and bake in the oven for about 20 to 25 minutes until golden and well risen. Serve warm with butter.

Doreen's Banana Bake

Doreen is a wonderful lady and cook I had the pleasure of working with at a children's home in Jersey. She has worked there for an incredible 22 years and has cooked this banana bake recipe of hers on numerous occasions, much to the delight of the many staff and children who have passed through her kitchen.

Preparation 15 minutes Cooking time 1 hour Makes 1 x 1kg (2lb) loaf
Cooking temperature 180°C, 350°F, gas mark 4
Equipment Large mixing bowl, 1kg (2lb) loaf tin, Scales, Electric whisk,
Fork for mashing the bananas, Teaspoon, Large mixing spoon, Wire cookie rack

Ingredients

100g (3¹/₂ oz) butter, at room
  temperature
2 eggs
100g (3¹/₂ oz) soft brown sugar
125g (4oz) wholemeal self-raising flour
1 teaspoon baking powder
2 bananas, mashed using the back
  of a fork
100g (3¹/₂ oz) sultanas
50g (2oz) chopped walnuts

Method

1. Pre-heat the oven to 180°C, 350°F, gas mark 4. Grease and line the bottom of a 1kg (2lb) loaf tin with baking paper.
2. Place the butter, eggs, soft brown sugar, flour and baking powder into a large bowl and whisk together well, using an electric whisk, until light and fluffy.
3. Fold in the banana, sultanas and walnuts. Pour into the prepared loaf tin and bake in the oven for about 1 hour. Cool on a wire rack.

Bugs Bunny Bake

We are using wholemeal self-raising flour in this traditional carrot cake, a healthier alternative. Wholemeal self-raising flour is not that easy to find in the shops, I buy mine from a health food shop.

Preparation 20 minutes **Cooking** 45-50 minutes **Makes** 10 to 12 portions
Oven temperature 180°C, 350°F, gas mark 4
Equipment Scales, Measuring jug, Peeler, Grater, Teaspoon, Knife, Large mixing bowl, Sieve, Electric whisk, 20cm (8inch) square or round cake tin, Scissors, Pastry brush, Wire rack, Palette knife, Baking paper

Ingredients

75g (3oz) butter, at room temperature
5 tablespoons sunflower oil
150g (5oz) soft brown sugar
2 eggs
125g (5oz) wholemeal self-raising flour
125g (5oz) self-raising flour
2 medium carrots, peeled and grated
1 teaspoon vanilla extract
2 bananas, mashed using back
   of a fork
2 tablespoons milk
100g (3 1/2 oz) walnuts, chopped
a little oil to grease

Topping

200g (7oz) low fat cream cheese
4 tablespoons icing sugar
1/2 teaspoon vanilla extract
extra walnuts or chocolate stars,
   to decorate

Method

1. Pre-heat the oven to 180°C, 350°F, gas mark 4. Lightly grease with oil and line the bottom of a 20cm (8inch) round or square cake tin with baking paper.

2. Place all of the cake ingredients into a large bowl and mix together well using an electric whisk. Pour into the prepared cake tin. Bake in the oven, on the middle shelf, for 45 to 50 minutes until golden and well risen. Allow to cool in the tin for 5 minutes, turn out onto a wire rack then leave to cool completely.

3. To make the topping place the cream cheese into a bowl. Sieve in the icing sugar and add the vanilla extract. Mix together until smooth. Spread on top of the cooled cake and make patterns using the back of a fork. Sprinkle with walnuts or chocolate stars and enjoy.

Chunky Chocolatey Cookies

Chocolate chip cookies have always been my favourite cookie, go on have a go at baking your own!

Preparation 15 minutes Cooking time 10 to 12 minutes Makes about 8 large cookies
Oven temperature 180°C, 350°F, gas mark 4
Equipment Scales, Teaspoon, Baking sheets, Pastry brush, Electric whisk, Tablespoon, Large bowl, Wire rack, Fish slice

Ingredients

120g (4oz) butter, at room
 temperature
250g (8oz) golden granulated sugar
1 egg
1 teaspoon vanilla extract
250g (8oz) plain flour
1 level teaspoon bicarbonate of soda
1 level teaspoon baking powder
50g (5oz) good quality white or milk
 chocolate, cut into big chunks
a little oil to grease

Method

1. Pre-heat the oven to 180°C, 350°F, gas mark 4. Grease some baking sheets. Using an electric whisk, cream together the butter and the sugar.
2. Still using the electric whisk, add the egg and vanilla extract.
3. Whisk in the flour, bicarbonate of soda and baking powder until you get a smooth creamy mixture. Stir in the chocolate chunks.
4. Drop tablespoonfuls of the mixture onto the baking sheets allowing plenty of room between each as they spread when cooking. Bake for 10 to 12 minutes, cool on a wire rack.

Chocolate, Chocolate, Chocolate Cheesecake

Your dreams are answered with our seriously chocolatey cheesecake. One thin slice will satisfy the biggest of chocoholics. Make, bake and enjoy!

Serves 10 to 12 chocoholics Preparation 20 minutes Cooking time 70 to 80 minutes
Oven temperature 170°C, 340°F, gas mark 3
Equipment Rolling pin, Large mixing bowl, 20cm (8inch) loose bottomed cake tin, Electric whisk, Large spoon, Baking sheet, Grater, Baking paper and a little oil to grease

Ingredients

Base

250g (8oz) chocolate digestive biscuits

125g (4oz) melted butter

Topping

400g (13oz) full fat cream cheese

75g (3oz) golden caster sugar

3 eggs

1 tablespoon cocoa powder

75g (3oz) good quality plain or milk chocolate, melted

50g (2oz) white chocolate, grated

Method

1. Preheat the oven to 170°C, 325°F, gas mark 3. Place the biscuits in a bag and bash them with a rolling pin until well crushed, mind your fingers! Melt the butter in a microwave, about 2 minutes, add the crushed biscuits and mix thoroughly.

2. Grease and line the bottom of the loose bottomed cake tin with baking paper. Put in the biscuit mixture and press down to cover the base.

3. Combine the cream cheese, sugar, eggs and cocoa powder with an electric whisk until smooth. Stir in the melted chocolate.

4. Pour onto the base and place on a baking sheet. Bake in the oven on the middle shelf for about 70 to 80 minutes, enough time to cook the eggs properly. Allow to cool and refrigerate over night in the tin. Turn out of the tin when ready to serve. Sprinkle with grated white chocolate and enjoy.

Mountain Munchies

Chocolate and banana flapjack

The energetic ingredients in the munchies will help you climb any mountain.

Makes 12 slices Preparation 15 minutes Oven temperature 180°C, 350°F, gas mark 4
Equipment Large bowl, Scales, Large spoon, Chopping board, Small bowl, Pastry brush,
Tablespoon, Knife, Baking parchment

Ingredients

150g (5oz) butter
5 tablespoons golden syrup
50g (2oz) light soft brown sugar
250g (8oz) porridge oats
300g (10oz) luxury muesli
3 bananas, sliced
1 tablespoon lemon juice
150g (5oz) good quality plain or milk
    chocolate, melted
a little oil to grease

Method

1. Pre-heat the oven to 180°C, 350°F, gas mark 4 and grease a 20 x 30cm (8 x 12inch) rectangular shallow ovenproof dish and line with baking parchment.
2. In a large bowl place the butter, golden syrup and sugar. Melt in a microwave until all the ingredients are dissolved and melted.
3. Stir in the porridge oats and muesli until well combined. In a separate bowl mix the sliced bananas and lemon juice.
4. Press half the porridge and muesli mixture into the prepared dish and spread the melted chocolate over the top. Arrange the sliced bananas over the chocolate. Spoon the rest of the porridge and muesli mixture over the top and gently press down.
5. Bake in the oven for about 30 minutes. Allow to stand for 5 minutes and then cut into 12 slices. Allow to cool completely before removing from the tin.

Little Sticky Toffee Puddings

A reinvented old classic recipe. By baking in individual muffin cases it makes them so much easier to prepare and serve.

Makes 10 puds **Preparation** 15 minutes **Oven temperature** 180°C, 350°F, gas mark 4
Equipment Muffin tray, Scales, Large bowl, Measuring jug, Tablespoon, Teaspoon, Knife, Small saucepan, Electric whisk

Ingredients

100g (3¹/₂oz) butter, at room
   temperature
160g (5¹/₂oz) light soft brown sugar
2 eggs
1 tablespoon coffee essence
200g (7oz) self-raising flour
1 tablespoon cocoa powder
1 teaspoon baking powder
160g (5¹/₂oz) stoned dates, roughly
   chopped
100g (3¹/₂oz) chopped walnuts
200ml (7floz) hot water

Toffee sauce

160g (5¹/₂oz) butter
160g (5¹/₂oz) light soft brown sugar
100g (3¹/₂oz) chopped walnuts
8 tablespoons double cream

Method

1. Pre-heat the oven to 180°C, 350°F, gas mark 4. Line a 12-hole muffin tray with 10 muffin paper cases.
2. Put the butter and sugar, eggs, coffee essence, flour, cocoa powder and baking powder into a large bowl and beat together with an electric whisk until well blended.
3. Stir in the dates, walnuts and hot water and pour this mixture into a jug. Pour into the muffin cases. Bake in the oven for 15 to 20 minutes until the puddings are well risen and golden.
4. While the puds cook make the sauce. Put the butter and sugar into a small saucepan, heat gently until the butter has melted and sugar dissolved. Stir in the walnuts and double cream and bring to the boil.
5. When the puds are cooked, remove the paper cases, place on a plate and spoon the sauce over the top. Serve and enjoy with ice cream or custard.

Lemon Heaven

This is a one stop easy and very quick lemon cake. The lemon juice icing gives it a zippy tangy taste sensation.

Makes 1 x 1kg (2lb) loaf Preparation 15 minutes Oven temperature 180°C, 350°F, gas mark 4
Cooking time 25 to 30 minutes
Equipment 1kg (2lb) loaf tin, Pastry brush, Large bowl, Electric whisk, Small bowl, Scales, Large spoon, Grater, Wire rack

Ingredients

Cake

100g (3¹/₂oz) butter, at room temperature
100g (3¹/₂oz) golden caster sugar
2 medium eggs
100g (3¹/₂oz) self-raising flower
grated rind of 1 lemon

Topping

lemon juice, squeezed from 1 lemon
icing sugar

Method

1. Pre-heat the oven to 180°C, 350°F, gas mark 4. Grease and line the bottom of a 1kg (2lb) loaf tin.
2. Place all the cake ingredients into a large bowl and beat together, using an electric whisk, until pale and fluffy. Place the mixture in the prepared loaf tin and bake for about 25 to 30 minutes until well risen and golden in colour. Cool on a wire rack.
3. For the topping squeeze the juice from the lemon into a bowl, add enough icing sugar to make a smooth glace icing. Pour over the cake when it's baked and cooled.

Key Lime Time

Key Lime pie is a traditional American treat, simple to make but extremely tasty. Limes contain useful amounts of vitamin C.

Serves 8 to 10 **Preparation** 20 minutes **Oven temperature** 175°C, 345°F, gas mark 4
Cooking time 25 minutes
Equipment 20cm (8inch) loose-bottomed cake tin, Large bowl, Large spoon, Rolling pin, Measuring jug, Baking sheet, Knife

Ingredients

Base

250g (8oz) digestive biscuits
   (about 15 biscuits)
125g (4oz) butter

Topping

6 egg yolks
2 x 400g tin sweetened
   condensed milk
200ml (7floz) lime juice

To Decorate

1 fresh lime, cut into slices
icing sugar, for dusting (optional)

Method

1. Preheat the oven to 190°C, 375°F, gas mark 5. Place the biscuits in a bag and bash with a rolling pin until well crushed. Melt the butter in a microwave, add the crushed biscuits and mix thoroughly.
2. Grease and line the bottom of the loose-bottomed cake tin with baking paper. Put in the biscuit mixture and press down to cover the base.
3. Combine the egg yolks, condensed milk and lime juice and blend by hand until it's smooth.
4. Pour onto the base, smooth out, place on a baking sheet and bake in the oven for about 25 minutes, just enough to cook the eggs properly. Allow to cool and refrigerate over night in the tin. Turn out of the tin and serve decorated with some lime slices, a little lime zest and a dusting of icing sugar if liked.

Honey Pot Rolls

Warm is the key word in this recipe. The yeast in bread responds best to warmth to make these brown bread rolls rise successfully. They are baked in terracotta flower pots which you can use over and over again to make unusual and attractive bread rolls.

Makes 6 Honey Pot Rolls Preparation 20 minutes Proving time 40-60 minutes
Cooking time 20 minutes Oven temperature 230°C, 450°F, gas mark 8
Equipment Large bowl, Teaspoon, Tablespoon, Baking sheet, Damp tea-towel,
6 clean terracotta flower pots about 8cm (3inches) tall, Pastry brush, Blunt knife

Ingredients

325g (11oz) granary malted brown
   bread flour
325g (11oz) strong white bread flour
2 teaspoons salt
1 teaspoon sugar
7g sachet fast acting yeast
200ml (7floz) milk
200ml (7floz) boiling water
3 tablespoons clear honey
1 tablespoon oil, to brush in the pots
a little extra white bread flour, to dust
1 tablespoon clear honey, to brush
   on top (that has been microwaved
   for 10 seconds)
3 tablespoons sunflower seeds

Method

1. Pre-heat the oven to 230°C, 450°F, gas mark 8. In a warm bowl sieve together the flours, tip the grains left in the sieve back in the bowl. Stir in the salt and sugar and the yeast.
2. Add the milk and water and clear honey. Mix to a soft dough and knead on a lightly floured work surface for 10 minutes.
3. Brush each terracotta pot with lots of warm oil and sprinkle with white bread flour then place on a baking sheet. Divide the dough evenly between the pots and cover with a warm, damp teatowel. Leave to stand in a warm place until the dough has doubled in size, about 40-60 minutes.
4. Cut slashes into the rolls, brush with warmed honey and sprinkle with sunflower seeds. Bake in the oven for about 20 minutes, allow to cool slightly and use a blunt knife to run around the inside of the pots to loosen the rolls, serve in the pots and enjoy.

A Piece Of Cake

This is a simply yummy double fudge cake. Using soft brown sugar in this recipe gives it a nice fudge flavour.

Makes 1 x 8 to 10 portion cake Oven temperature 180°C, 350°F, gas mark 4
Cooking time 20 minutes Preparation 20 minutes
Equipment 2 x 18cm (7inch) round cake tins, Pastry brush, Scales, Large mixing bowl, Electric whisk, Tablespoon, Teaspoon, Palette knife, Scissors, Wire rack, Baking paper

Ingredients

Cake

150g (5oz) self-raising flour

2 level tablespoons cocoa powder

150g (5oz) butter, at room
    temperature

150g (5oz) soft brown sugar

3 eggs

3 tablespoons milk

For the icing

50g (2oz) butter, at room
    temperature

3 tablespoons golden syrup

1 tablespoon cocoa powder

200g (7oz) icing sugar

50g (2oz) cream cheese

To decorate

chocolate sprinkles

Method

1. Pre-heat the oven to 180°C, 350°F, gas mark 4. Grease and line the bottoms of two 18cm (7inch) round cake tins with baking paper.

2. Place all of the cake ingredients into a large bowl and whisk together using an electric whisk until light and fluffy. Pour into the prepared tins and bake in the oven for about 20 minutes, until risen and golden. Leave in the tins to cool for 10 minutes and then transfer to a wire rack to cool completely.

3. To make the icing whisk together all the icing ingredients until smooth. Spread the icing in the middle of the two sponges, sandwich together and spread the rest all over the top. Top with chocolate sprinkles.

Mighty Mars Muffins

By placing slices of a Mars Bar over the top of hot muffins you get a delicious gooey sensation.

Makes 12 muffins **Preparation** 20 minutes **Oven temperature** 200°C, 400°F, gas mark 6
Cooking time 15 to 20 minutes
Equipment Muffin tray, Paper muffin cases, Large bowl, Scales, Large mixing spoon, Knife, Teaspoon, Tablespoon, Measuring jug, Electric whisk

Ingredients

75g (3oz) butter, at room temperature
250g (8oz) light soft brown sugar
100g (4oz) good quality plain chocolate
200ml (7floz) milk
2 eggs
1 level tablespoon cocoa powder
175g (6oz) self-raising flour
1 teaspoon bicarbonate of soda
4 Mars Bars, thinly sliced

Method

1. Pre-heat the oven to 200°C, 400°F, gas mark 6. Line a 12-section muffin tray with paper cases. Place the butter, sugar and chocolate in a large bowl and heat in a microwave. About 2 to 3 minutes, stirring at intervals. Allow to cool slightly.
1. Measure the milk into a jug, add the eggs and beat using a fork. Add to the chocolate mixture with the cocoa powder, flour and bicarbonate of soda. Mix with an electric whisk until well blended. Pour back into the jug and pour into the paper cases.
1. Bake in the oven for about 15 to 20 minutes until well risen. Arrange the sliced Mars Bars over the top of the still hot muffins.

Enjoy warm and gooey!

Party
Pick Ups

Nacho Nibbles

A really tasty way with nachos but they do need to be served straight away; left to cool they go soggy.

Preparation 10 minutes Cooking time 5 minutes
Oven temperature 200°C, 400°F, gas mark 6
Equipment Baking sheet, Tablespoon, Bowl, Teaspoon, Knife, Grater

Ingredients
1 tablespoon olive oil
1 teaspoon garlic puree
300ml (10floz) tomato passata
1 tablespoon sweet chilli sauce
1 tablespoon lemon juice
1 handful chopped fresh coriander, plus
   a little extra to serve
100g (3¹/₂oz) original corn tortilla
   chips (whole, not broken)
50g (2oz) grated cheese (any variety)
salt and pepper

Method
1. Pre-heat the oven to 200°C, 400°F, gas mark 6. Grease a large baking sheet. Heat the oil in a saucepan, add the garlic and cook for 1 minute.
2. Add the passata, chilli sauce and lemon juice. Cook simmering for 15 minutes, season to taste. Add the chopped coriander and stir.
3. Place the nachos on the greased baking sheet. Put a teaspoon of the sauce onto the nachos. Sprinkle each with grated cheese and bake in the oven for about 5 minutes, until the cheese is melted and bubbling. Serve straight away with a sprig of fresh coriander on each.

Pesto Pick Ups Chicken & tomato bits

You could use a tomato pasta sauce instead of pesto, the choice is yours.

Preparation 15 minutes Cooking time 15 minutes
Oven temperature 200°C, 400°F, gas mark 6
Equipment Baking sheet, Knife, Chopping board, Grater, Teaspoon

Ingredients

2 boneless, skinless chicken breasts
    (about 200g/7oz)
100g (3½oz) pesto sauce
50g (2oz) grated cheese (any type you
    fancy, I used mozzarella)
10 cherry tomatoes cut into slices
basil leaves to decorate

Method

1. Pre-heat the oven to 200°C, 400°F, gas mark 6.
   Lightly grease a baking sheet.
2. Slice the chicken breasts lengthways down the
   middle so you have two large thin slices. Slice each
   of those into 6 fairly even-sized portions, giving
   you 12 pieces of chicken.
3. Place the chicken onto the greased baking sheet.
   With a teaspoon, spoon some pesto onto each
   piece of chicken. Sprinkle with grated cheese and a
   slice of cherry tomato.
4. Cook in the oven for about 15 minutes until the
   cheese is golden and bubbling and the chicken is
   cooked through. Serve decorated with a few fresh
   basil leaves hot or cold and enjoy.

Little
mouthfuls
of yumminess!

Pick Up Porkers

Cocktail sausages with a lovely honey sauce – a great way to jazz up sausages.

Preparation 5 minutes Cooking time 30 minutes
Oven temperature 200°C, 400°F, gas mark 6
Equipment Baking sheet, Tablespoon, Bowl

Ingredients

500g (16oz) cocktail sausages
   (I use frozen ones)
1 tablespoon clear honey
2 tablespoons Worcestershire sauce
1 tablespoon soy sauce
2 tablespoons tomato ketchup

Method

1. Pre-heat the oven to 200°C, 400°F, gas mark 6. Lightly grease a baking sheet. Mix all the ingredients together in a bowl, except the sausages.
2. Place the sausages in the sauce and coat really well.
3. Tip the sausages onto the baking sheet with the sauce. Cook the sausages according to the packet instructions, my frozen ones take 30 minutes, spooning the sauce over the sausages from time to time. Serve hot or cold with cocktail sticks.

Potato Pick Ups Home-made crisps

Fifty per cent of 8 to 15 year-olds are eating at least one packet of crisps a day and just by eating crisps alone half of all the children in the UK are consuming 5 litres of cooking oil a year. So make your own healthy variety.

Preparation 15 minutes **Cooking time** 30 to 40 minutes
Oven temperature 150°C, 300°F, gas mark 2
Equipment Chopping board, 3 baking sheets, Peeler, Bowl to serve

Ingredients

1 medium potato

1 small sweet potato

1 medium parsnip

sunflower oil spray

salt to season

Method

1. Pre-heat the oven to 150°C, 300°F, gas mark 2. Wash and dry the vegetables, top and tail the sweet potato and parsnip.
2. Using a peeler, firstly peel the skin off all the vegetables. Then peel the sweet potato and potato into strips randomly in any direction until they are completely peeled away. Peel the parsnip in the same way but stop when you reach the woody centre. Throw this away. Keep the vegetables in separate batches. Dry them on kitchen paper.
3. Spray 3 baking trays with sunflower oil spray. Spread the vegetables onto the 3 trays in a single layer and spray with sunflower spray. Bake in the oven for 30 to 40 minutes, turning from time-to-time until they are evenly crisp and golden. Some may be ready before others so take them out as they cook. Place on a wire rack and cool and sprinkle with a little salt when ready to serve.

Stick-a-Choca Glory

This is a delicious combination of fresh fruit and tasty chocolate sauce.

Cooking time 2 minutes Makes 1kg (2lb)of fruit
Preparation 10 minutes
Equipment Chopping board, Knife, Small saucepan, Large spoon

Ingredients

250ml (8floz) double cream

150g (5oz) good quality plain, white or milk chocolate, broken into chunks

a mixture of any kind of fruit; berries, peach slices, pineapple chunks, chunks of banana, wedges of kiwi, grapes

marshmallows

Method

1. Bring the cream just to the boil in a small pan and take off the heat. Stir in the chocolate and stir until smooth and the chocolate has melted. Allow to cool.

2. Arrange your fruit and marshmallows in glasses or on kebab sticks or in a pile to be picked up by cocktail sticks.

3. Pour the chocolate sauce over the glasses of fruit or kebab sticks. Or place the sauce in a bowl so that the fruit can be dunked in with a cocktail stick, the choice is yours!

Jelly Belly & Ice Cream

Homemade fruit jelly with yoghurt and fruit juice ice cream

Good old-fashioned jelly and ice cream? No this one is a showstopper. It looks fantastic, tastes delicious and there are lots of nutritional benefits in the summer fruits containing lots of vitamin C and fibre. Using frozen summer fruits you can dish up this jelly all year round – go on and show off to your friends and family.

Serves 6 to 8 Preparation 10 minutes plus an hour to cool down the grape drink and over night refrigeration
Equipment 1/2 litre jelly mould or bowl, Strainer, Large bowl, 1 ice-cube tray, Small saucepan, Hand whisk, Tablespoon, Large spoon, Serving plate

Ingredients

Jelly

500g (16oz) frozen summer fruits

500ml (18floz) sparkling white grape drink

1 x 11g sachet gelatine

Ice cream

2 x 125g (5oz) smooth strawberry or raspberry yoghurts

Method

1. Defrost the fruit in a strainer over a bowl and reserve the juice. Pour the juice into an ice-cube tray to fill each section one third full with the juice. Place in the freezer to freeze.
2. In a small saucepan bring the white grape drink to the boil and whisk in the gelatine. Set to one side to cool.
3. Tip the fruit into the cooled grape drink and gently stir. Pour half into a jelly mould or suitably sized bowl. Refrigerate for about 2 hours or until the top has set.
4. Warm through the remaining liquid and fruit and stir, pour over the jelly. Doing this in two halves will distribute the fruit throughout the jelly and it won't all float to the top. Refrigerate overnight.
5. When the fruit juice has frozen in the ice-cube tray, take out of the freezer and fill each section with the strawberry or raspberry yoghurt and return to the freezer.
6. The next day when ready to serve dip the jelly mould carefully and quickly into hot water and turn out the jelly onto a plate. Take the ice-cube tray out of the freezer about 15 minutes before it's needed and allow to stand prior to pressing out the yoghurt ice creams. Serve.

Sunray Sorbet **Strawberry sorbet**

**Cool down those hot summer days with this refreshing sorbet.
It's so simple to make and simply delicious.**

Serves 4 to 6 Preparation 10 minutes, with 3 to 4 hour refrigeration
Equipment Liquidiser, Plastic freezer container, Scales

Ingredients

500g (16oz) fresh strawberries
100ml (3floz) water
50g (2oz) caster sugar
**a few extra strawberries and fresh mint
    leaves, to serve**

Method

1. Liquidise the strawberries, water and sugar
   together until smooth.
2. Pour into a plastic container and cover.
   Place in the freezer until firm enough to scoop out.
   This will take about 3 to 4 hours approximately.
   Serve decorated with some whole strawberries and
   mint leaves.

Summer Superbowls Iced flower bowls

This has definitely got the wow factor. Used at any party filled with lollies, ice cream or fruit it will definitely have your friends and family admiring your skills.

Preparation 10 minutes, freeze overnight
Equipment 2 large bowls, (One bowl slightly smaller than the other), Pebbles or stones, Knife for slicing the fruit, Chopping board, Plastic bag

Ingredients

Fruity bowls

thinly sliced oranges
thinly sliced lemons
thinly sliced limes
mint leaves

Flower bowls

cut flowers and leaves
water

To serve

Ice cubes
ice cream
fruit lollies

Method

1. Half fill the larger bowl with water. Place the smaller bowl inside. Fill a bag with enough pebbles to weigh down the smaller bowl so that the water rises up the side of the larger bowl to the top. There should be about 1cm to 2cm (1 inch) of water all around. The small bowl should not be touching the bottom of the larger bowl, it should be floating slightly.
2. Arrange the cut flowers or fruit and leaves or fruit in the water between the 2 bowls.
3. Place completely flat in a freezer and allow to freeze overnight.
4. When you are ready to use the ice bowl take it out of the freezer and allow to stand until the bowls leave the ice easily. Do not force or dip into water or it will crack. Use immediately. Fill with ice, ice cream, lollies or fruit.

All Shook Up Shake

Makes 2 smoothies

Ingredients

200g (7oz) raspberries, fresh, frozen
    or tinned
300g (10oz) natural yoghurt
500ml (18floz) milk
2 tablespoons caster sugar

Method

1. Place all of the ingredients into a liquidiser and blend until smooth. Serve in tall glasses. If in this recipe you use frozen raspberries you will get a lovely slushy texture.

Pineapple Punch

Makes 2 drinks

Ingredients

1 small tin 227g (9oz) of pineapple
    with juice
250ml (8floz) fresh orange juice
400ml (16floz) good quality lemonade

Method

1. Crush the pineapple in a liquidiser. Add the orange juice and lemonade. Pour in tall glasses over crushed ice.

Index